Put Beginning Readers on the Right Track with
ALL ABOARD READING™

The All Aboard Reading series is especially designed for beginning readers. Written by noted authors and illustrated in full color, these are books that children really want to read—books to excite their imagination, expand their interests, make them laugh, and support their feelings. With fiction and nonfiction stories that are high interest and curriculum-related, All Aboard Reading books offer something for every young reader. And with four different reading levels, the All Aboard Reading series lets you choose which books are most appropriate for your children and their growing abilities.

Picture Readers
Picture Readers have super-simple texts, with many nouns appearing as rebus pictures. At the end of each book are 24 flash cards—on one side is a rebus picture; on the other side is the written-out word.

Station Stop 1
Station Stop 1 books are best for children who have just begun to read. Simple words and big type make these early reading experiences more comfortable. Picture clues help children to figure out the words on the page. Lots of repetition throughout the text helps children to predict the next word or phrase—an essential step in developing word recognition.

Station Stop 2
Station Stop 2 books are written specifically for children who are reading with help. Short sentences make it easier for early readers to understand what they are reading. Simple plots and simple dialogue help children with reading comprehension.

Station Stop 3
Station Stop 3 books are perfect for children who are reading alone. With longer text and harder words, these books appeal to children who have mastered basic reading skills. More complex stories captivate children who are ready for more challenging books.

In addition to All Aboard Reading books, look for All Aboard Math Readers™ (fiction stories that teach math concepts children are learning in school) and All Aboard Science Readers™ (nonfiction books that explore the most fascinating science topics in age-appropriate language).

All Aboard for happy reading!

To my dad, Stan, a World War II soldier;
and Megan, for all her help. Thanks—G.T.

To Andrew and Peter—L.D.

Special thanks to Beverly McMillan.

Text copyright © 2003 by Gare Thompson. Illustrations copyright © 2003 by Larry Day.
All rights reserved. Published by Grosset & Dunlap, a division of Penguin Young Readers
Group, 345 Hudson Street, New York, NY 10014. GROSSET & DUNLAP is a trademark of
Penguin Group (USA) Inc. Published simultaneously in Canada. The scanning, uploading
and distribution of this book via the Internet or via any other means without the permission
of the publisher is illegal and punishable by law. Please purchase only authorized electronic
editions, and do not participate in or encourage electronic piracy of copyrighted materials.
Your support of the author's rights is appreciated.

Library of Congress Cataloging-in-Publication Data is available.

ISBN 0-448-43245-5 (pbk)   A B C D E F G H I J
ISBN 0-448-43283-8 (GB)   A B C D E F G H I J

THE MONITOR

The Iron Warship that Changed the World

By Gare Thompson
Illustrated by Larry Day

Grosset & Dunlap • New York

Chapter 1

Deep in the Atlantic Ocean, a mystery awaits. The mystery is the *Monitor*, an ironclad warship that sank on New Year's Eve, 1862. For over 100 years, the *Monitor* has rested in a silent grave. Sand buries part of the ship. Where sailors once worked, fish now swim. And no one in the world knows where the *Monitor* lies.

Then, in 1973, the silence of the deep is broken. Using old records and modern technology, scientists think they may have finally found the *Monitor*. The team searches an area called the "Graveyard of the Atlantic" because so many ships have sunk there. Finding the *Monitor* among all of those other shipwrecks won't be easy. But the team is determined to try.

Why was it so important to find the *Monitor*? What makes this ship stand out among all the other wrecks in the area? What secrets are hidden within its iron hull?

The answers lie in the lost ship's history—and in the ship itself.

Chapter 2

It is December 1860, and the United States is about to break apart in a terrible civil war. People from the South want to start their own country. People from the North want the nation to stay together. This is only one issue that the North and the South argue about. Another one is slavery. Many people in the South have slaves that work on their plantations. Many people in the North want to end slavery. The two sides cannot agree. One by one, Southern states leave the United States to start a new nation, the Confederacy.

In 1861, the war begins.

President Abraham Lincoln wants the United States to stay together. And he wants the war to end soon. The North

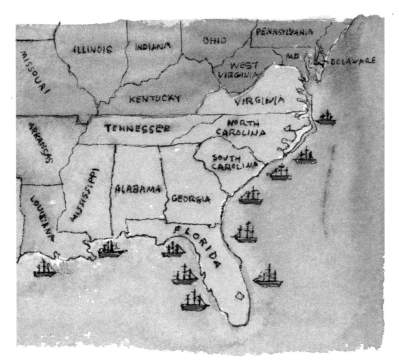

Confederate States

believes it can win the war by blocking Southern ports with fast wooden warships. This <u>blockade</u> will keep supplies and guns from reaching the South. Without supplies, the North hopes, the South will be forced to surrender.

The South knows that a blockade could make them lose the war. But what can the South do about all of the North's wooden warships? Stephen Mallory is in charge of the Confederate navy. He has heard of a new kind of ship—the ironclad—that is being built in Europe. These ships are covered with iron. They are stronger and more powerful than ships that are made only of wood. And they are very hard to damage. Mallory believes that an ironclad ship could break through the blockade.

But the South doesn't have enough time, money, or iron to build a whole ironclad from scratch. Mallory figures out a way to solve this problem. Instead of building a new ship, the South will turn a wooden warship into an ironclad. They cover a captured Northern ship, the *Merrimac*, with thick iron plates. It is slow, hard work. But it will be worth it.

Northern spies hear about the South's ironclad and report back to the United States government. Gideon Welles, the man in charge of the Northern navy, knows that a Southern ironclad is bad news for the North. It could easily destroy many Northern ships. There is only one thing to do: The North must build its own ironclad. There isn't a moment to lose.

Many engineers design ironclads for the North, but only one ship will be built. One man, John Ericsson, has been dreaming of building an ironclad for over 25 years. Welles likes Ericsson's model the best. So does President Lincoln. For Ericsson, it is a dream come true! On October 25, 1861, the Navy begins building his ironclad, the *Monitor*, in New York.

When the South finds out about the North's plans, they resolve to finish their ironclad first. They rename the ship the *Virginia* and work on it day and night.

The North and South race to build their ironclads because of Hampton Roads, an important waterway for ships. If the South takes control of Hampton Roads, they would be able to break the blockade—and attack Washington, D.C., the U.S. capital. If the North takes control of Hampton Roads, they could keep the blockade strong. They could

Iron plates

The *Merrimac's* original hull

also attack Richmond, Virginia, the capital of the Confederacy.

Both sides are building ironclads, but their ships are very different. The *Virginia* is huge—275 feet long! It has eight large cannons, four on each side. Workers cover the top half of the wooden ship with three inches of iron. One of the scariest parts of the ship is its large ram.

The *Virginia*

Shaped like a giant arrow, it juts out from the *Virginia's* bow and is used to make huge holes in the sides of enemy ships. The ships then fill with water and sink.

While the *Virginia* is large, the *Monitor* is small. It is only 173 feet long. But the *Monitor* has some important advantages over the *Virginia*. Most of the ship is below the waterline. There, the crew will be safe from enemy gunfire. The *Monitor* also has a gun turret that turns in a circle. Most ships, including the *Virginia*, have

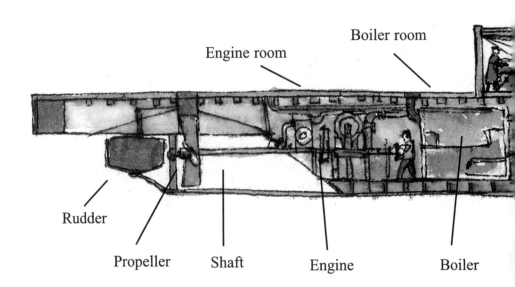

Boiler room

Engine room

Rudder

Propeller

Shaft

Engine

Boiler

cannons on their sides. The ships have to turn to point their guns in a different direction. But the *Monitor's* gun turret turns while the ship stays in one place. It can aim and shoot faster—and hit moving ships!

Every day, Ericsson goes to the dock-yard where the *Monitor* is being built. The smell of iron fills the air as men work around the clock to finish the iron-clad. To most people, the low ship looks like it is about to sink. The workers have

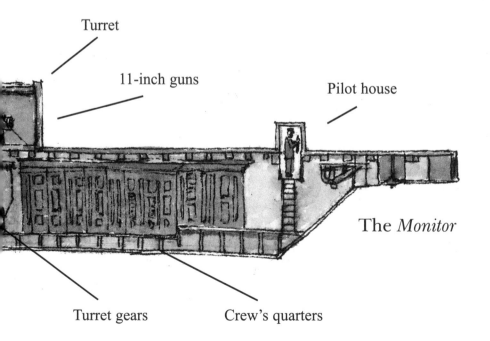

Turret

11-inch guns

Pilot house

The *Monitor*

Turret gears   Crew's quarters

doubts about the ironclad, too. The gun turret looks too big. The deck seems too small. Will this strange ship even float?

When the *Monitor* is finished, crowds gather on the docks to watch the ironclad launch on January 30, 1862. People have never seen anything like it. Some call it an "iron coffin" because they are sure it will sink. A rescue boat waits nearby—just in case. Slowly, the *Monitor* moves out of the harbor.

It doesn't sink. The crowd cheers!

When leaders in the South learn that the North's ironclad is on the move, they quickly launch the *Virginia*, even though it's not finished yet. It is worth the risk. Both sides are racing to Hampton Roads.

Who will get there first?

Chapter 3

Slowly, the *Monitor* makes its way to Hampton Roads. Captain John Worden leads 58 crewmen to protect the ships there. The first day and night at sea are calm. But the winter weather in the Atlantic Ocean is dangerous. It can change in an instant. And it does.

A fierce storm hits the *Monitor*. Its low deck fills with water. Waves crash over the pilothouse with such force that a man is knocked over. There is a leak in the gun turret. The workers who doubted Ericsson's design did not follow his orders. Now the crew is paying for this mistake. They are in great danger.

Then, things get worse.

The *Monitor* has a steam engine to make it move. Funnels from the steam

engine let smoke out. Fans bring fresh air
in. But now waves pour down the funnels
and flood the engine room. The fans stop.
The engine shuts down. Poisonous fumes
fill the ship. The crewmen, gasping for
air, crawl to the deck. Huge waves crash
over them as they try to breathe.

Captain Worden orders the crew to
start bailing by pouring buckets of

seawater over the sides. At last, the storm
dies down, and five long hours later, the
Monitor is in calm seas. Sailors fix the
engine and fans. Miraculously, the
Monitor is on its way again. But the storm
has cost them time.

While the *Monitor* struggles in the
storm, the *Virginia* steams down the
Elizabeth River toward Hampton Roads.
Captain Franklin Buchanan is eager to
test the ironclad in battle. On March 8,
1862, the *Virginia* arrives in Hampton
Roads. There are two Northern ships
there—the *Cumberland* and the *Congress*—
that are important to the blockade. The
Virginia plans to destroy them both.

Northern sailors on the ships see a
plume of black smoke rising in the dis-
tance. It is the South's ironclad! They
have almost no time to get ready for this

surprise attack. Soon the mighty *Virginia*
is upon them.

The *Virginia's* first target is the
Cumberland. The wooden ship splinters
where one of the *Virginia's* cannonballs
hits it. The *Cumberland* fires back, but its
shots do not stop the *Virginia*. The
Virginia's second shot kills many of the
Cumberland's gun crew. The sailors of
the *Cumberland* can do nothing to stop the

metal monster approaching them.

Then the *Virginia* smashes the *Cumberland* with its powerful ram, ripping a seven-foot hole in it. Seawater pours in, and the ship pitches over. The *Cumberland's* brave crew continues to fight, but the ship is doomed. Finally, the captain of the *Cumberland* orders his men to abandon ship—before they all drown.

The *Congress* has watched the fearsome

attack on the *Cumberland*. The captain of
the *Congress* runs his ship aground so that
it is out of reach of the *Virginia's* ram. But
Captain Buchanan is determined to
destroy the *Congress*. He orders his crew
to heat cannonballs in a fire until they
are red-hot. When they hit the *Congress*,
the wooden ship bursts into flame.
Before the sailors abandon ship, though,
one of them fires a gun at Captain

Buchanan and hits him in the leg. As
Captain Buchanan is carried below deck,
Lieutenant Jones takes over, but the battle
is nearly finished. With one Northern
ship at the bottom of the sea and another
burning on the shore, the South has
easily won.

Then, another Northern ship, the
Minnesota, arrives. The *Virginia* fires, but
is too far away to hit it. Shallow water

keeps the *Virginia* from moving closer, so Lt. Jones orders the *Virginia* back to port as darkness falls on Hampton Roads.

All night, the *Cumberland* burns, lighting the sky. The battle was a terrible blow for the Northern navy. The South's ironclad is more dangerous than anyone expected. There is only one hope for the sailors at Hampton Roads—the *Monitor*.

Luckily, the *Monitor* soon arrives to protect the *Minnesota*. The crew is tired from the long, dangerous trip. They have not slept for days. Captain Worden talks to his crew. He knows they are scared and worried. He tells them that he is proud of them and that they will fight well tomorrow. Even so, few men sleep that night.

The two ironclads are set to battle. Which one will win?

The next morning, a tower of black

smoke appears on the Elizabeth River. It is the *Virginia*, heading straight for the *Minnesota*! At 8:30 A.M. on March 9, 1862, the battle begins.

No one knows who fires the first shot. Most believe that the *Virginia* fires first on the *Minnesota*. Though the *Minnesota* is hit and slightly damaged, it fires back. But its cannonballs do little harm to the *Virginia*. It looks like the *Minnesota* is doomed. But the *Monitor* joins the battle just in time, and Captain Worden pilots the ship in front of the *Minnesota* to protect it. The two ironclads fire cannonballs back and forth. But neither ship is seriously damaged.

On shore, over 20,000 people gather to watch the battle—including hundreds of soldiers. The Northern army fires on the *Virginia*, but the bullets do not stop the ship. The cannons roar like thunder.

Smoke fills the harbor. The battle rages on and on. Heavy cannonballs that would have destroyed any wooden ship in the world only dent the ironclads.

In the *Monitor's* pilothouse, Captain Worden watches the battle and shouts orders to his crew. He peers out the pilothouse's narrow window, trying to get a better view of the *Virginia*.

SMASH!

A cannonball hits the pilothouse, right where Captain Worden stands! Miraculously, he survives, but splinters of metal pierce his eyeballs and blind him. Below deck, the ship doctor tries to remove the splinters. Captain Worden will later regain his sight, but he cannot lead the *Monitor* now. Lieutenant Greene takes command and steers the *Monitor* away. The crew needs time to recover from the blow.

Meanwhile, the *Virginia* tries to attack the *Minnesota*. But it cannot get close enough to fire because the water is too shallow. The two ironclads have been fighting for over three hours with no end in sight.

Suddenly, the *Virginia* springs a leak from one of the many hits it has taken. The ship retreats to the Elizabeth River. The *Monitor's* crew cheers. The battle is finally over!

But who won?

Both sides claim victory. The *Virginia* hurt the blockade. And it is clearly a serious threat to the North. But the *Monitor* protected the *Minnesota*. It stopped the *Virginia's* terrible attack. The blockade is still strong. And the North still has control of Hampton Roads.

After the battle, one reporter wrote,

"iron will be the king of the seas." He was right. The clash forever changed how ships fight at sea. Countries stopped building wooden ships and built this new type of ship, called monitors. Only five days after the battle, the Northern navy ordered six more ironclads to be built. The powerful design of the little *Monitor* led to the huge battleships of today.

Chapter 4

What happened to the *Monitor* and the
Virginia after their fierce battle? The two
ships never fought again. In May 1862,
the Northern army captured Norfolk,
Virginia, where the *Virginia* was stationed.
The crew of the *Virginia* did not want the
North to have their prize ship. So they
blew it up before they fled the city.

Meanwhile, the *Monitor* steamed up and
down the coast, firing at Southern forts. It
never went to battle again. Like the South,
the North did not want its powerful ironclad to fall into enemy hands.

But on Christmas Day, 1862, the
Monitor was ordered to go to Beaufort,
North Carolina. The ship would become
part of the Northern blockade there. The

new captain, John Bankhead, and his crew were worried about the trip. The North Carolina coast was often stormy. The sailors remembered how the *Monitor* had almost sunk during a storm on its first voyage. The crew decided to have the *Monitor* towed by a big, powerful steamer called the *Rhode Island*—just in case a storm hit.

The two ships sailed out on December 29, 1862. The sky was clear and the sea was calm. But the next day, the wind picked up. Captain Bankhead was concerned. He sent a message to the *Rhode Island* that if the *Monitor* needed help, he would hang a red lantern.

That night, rough seas tossed the *Monitor*. Gigantic waves knocked the crew off their feet. And to make matters worse, all the lifeboats had been moved to the

Rhode Island. If the *Monitor's* crew needed to abandon ship, they would have to wait to be rescued by the *Rhode Island*.

On the *Monitor*, the sailors tried desperately to save the ship. They bailed water, but it came in faster than they could get it out. Soon, there was over a foot of water in the ironclad! As the *Monitor* struggled in the raging seas, it put the *Rhode Island* at risk. Captain Bankhead knew that the *Monitor* could sink and take the *Rhode*

Island with it. So he ordered the tow rope
to be cut. The two sailors who went to cut
the rope were washed overboard. They
disappeared into the black, swirling sea—
and drowned.

Finally, Captain Bankhead gave up on
saving the ship. A sailor hung a red lantern
from the gun turret of the *Monitor*.

Rescue boats set off from the *Rhode
Island*, bobbing like apples in the raging

sea. The sailors were terrified—but they
were determined to save the *Monitor's* crew.

When the lifeboats from the *Rhode Island*
arrived, Captain Bankhead ordered the
crew off the *Monitor*. The water in the
ironclad was now waist-deep. Most of the
crew scrambled into rowboats. But some
men clung to the turret. The small rowboats were so full that they seemed in danger of sinking, too! Captain Bankhead told

the men to get into the rowboats, but they refused. They felt it was safer to wait for another round of rescue boats.

This decision would cost them their lives.

Waves tossed the tiny rowboats as the men clung to the sides. At last, they made it to the *Rhode Island*. A huge wave smashed one of the lifeboats just as the *Rhode Island's* crew dragged the men aboard. Another rowboat was sent back to the *Monitor* for the sailors who still clung to the gun turret. It was almost there when, suddenly, the *Monitor*, the red lantern, and the men disappeared into the dark waters. Sixteen men drowned that night, lost with the iron-clad beneath the ocean waves.

Chapter 5

The *Monitor* was gone, but not forgotten. As the years passed, people kept searching for the ship. Yet without knowing exactly where the *Monitor* had sunk, it seemed impossible to find.

In 1973, two people started searching for the *Monitor* in a different way. Gordon Watts and Dorothy Nicholson knew the *Rhode Island* had towed the ironclad. By reading the *Rhode Island's* record book and recreating the ship's route, they believed they could find the *Monitor*.

Watts and Nicholson studied maps and charts of the Atlantic Ocean. These documents gave them more clues about where the *Monitor* had sunk. They made their own maps and charts. Finally, they

concluded that the *Monitor* must have
sunk in Hatteras, off the coast of North
Carolina.

In August 1973, a group of scientists
set out for Hatteras on a ship called
the *Eastward*. They used the map that
Watts and Nicholson had created. Like a
treasure map, *X* marked the spot where
they hoped to find the *Monitor*.

The scientists brought along a lot of equipment. Underwater cameras, sonar devices, and television monitors would help them find the ship, but it would not be easy. They had to search 96 square miles of ocean floor and the hundreds of shipwrecks that lay in the "Graveyard of the Atlantic."

By the end of the first week, the

scientists had found 21 possible ships.
One of the most important tools they
used was sonar. Sonar sends sound waves
through the ocean. The sound waves
bounce off objects on the ocean floor
and make patterns on a screen. Scientists
can tell the size of the objects from the
patterns. Most of the 21 objects at
Hatteras were the wrong size. But one

was the right size—and the right shape. Had they finally found the *Monitor*?

No, it was just part of another ship.

As the days passed, the scientists began to lose hope. Would they ever find the *Monitor*? Then, a funny accident gave them an important clue. One of the scientists, Fred Kelly, decided to go fishing. He used the sonar to look for fish in the ocean. To

his surprise, the sonar found something more than fish—something that looked like it might be the *Monitor*. He showed it to the other scientists. What was it? They took a closer look.

The scientists sent down a sensitive underwater camera. It showed the outline of a shipwreck. Even more amazing was what seemed to be the famous gun turret resting upside down on the deck. The shapes of the ship and the turret matched the *Monitor* exactly! The scientists cheered. They were sure that they had solved the mystery of where the *Monitor* had sunk!

In 1974, a research ship, the *Alcoa Seaprobe*, went back to the site of the shipwreck to take more photos. Like pieces of a giant puzzle, scientists put the photos together until they had a complete

picture of the *Monitor*. More questions
arose with the photographs. For instance,
why was the *Monitor* broken into two
pieces? Scientists believe that when the
ship hit the ocean floor, the gun turret
fell onto the deck.

After so many years in the ocean, the
Monitor was in bad shape. Decay caused

by seawater had made the ship's strong iron as fragile as glass. The ship could fall apart if it was moved. Since the *Monitor* could not be safely brought to the surface, it had to be protected where it was. In 1975, scientists convinced Congress to make the shipwreck a marine sanctuary. That meant that no one could explore or disturb the *Monitor* without permission.

But as time passed, scientists realized that the harsh conditions in the ocean could completely destroy the *Monitor*. Bit by bit, divers brought parts of the ironclad, including its engine and anchor, to the surface. But the real challenge would be raising the gun turret. Could they do it?

Chapter 6

John Broadwater, director of the
Monitor National Marine Sanctuary,
knew that the *Monitor's* gun turret was
like a sunken treasure. He wanted to
bring that treasure to the surface before it
was destroyed and lost forever. Working
with Commander Bobbie Scholley of the
Navy's Mobile Diving and Salvage Unit,
he came up with a plan.

A team of over 150 divers and scientists
worked together to raise the gun turret.
A huge barge floated near the sunken
ship. Divers attached a giant, eight-legged
claw called a "spider" to the gun turret.
They began to slowly lift it to the surface.
Finally, on August 9, 2002, the gun turret
broke through the surface. It was placed

on the waiting barge. A parade of ships brought the turret to The Mariners' Museum in Newport News, Virginia, where a 21-gun salute greeted its arrival. Hundreds of people came to watch the *Monitor's* gun turret return to Virginia.

After being in the ocean for so long, the gun turret was full of mud. Workers used a pump to remove it. The inside of the turret was cold and damp. Even after spending years underwater, it still smelled

like coal! Scientists say it will take about ten years to fully clean the gun turret. It will then be coated with a special liquid to protect it from moisture. Like detectives, the workers sift carefully through the silt, searching for artifacts. So far, they have found buttons, coins, pocketknives, and a wool coat. They also found a wedding ring and a silver piece with initials carved on it. All of these items help paint a picture of what life was like on the ship.

The most important finds inside the gun turret were two human bones, which were sent to a laboratory in Hawaii. There, scientists will study them and try to identify them. Then the bones will be returned to the relatives of the lost crew for a burial ceremony.

Every day, scientists learn more about life on the *Monitor*. Even though they are not finished excavating the gun turret, it is on display at The Mariners' Museum—not far from where the *Monitor* fought the *Virginia*. Today, everyone can see this important part of the *Monitor*—the amazing ironclad that changed the world!